WOKING TO SOUTHAMPTON

Vic Mitchell and Keith Smith

Design – Deborah Goodridge

First published May 1988

ISBN 0 906520 55 X

© Middleton Press, 1988

Typeset by CitySet - Bosham 573270

Published by Middleton Press
    Easebourne Lane
    Midhurst, West Sussex
    GU29 9AZ
    ☎ (073 081) 3169

Printed & bound by Biddles Ltd,
    Guildford and Kings Lynn

Cover: A westbound freight passes under the air operated signals at Basingstoke on 25th July 1965. Steam still reigned supreme then, as class S15 no.30843 faces the climb to Worting Junction. (E. Wilmshurst)

CONTENTS

ACKNOWLEDGEMENTS

In addition to the many photographers mentioned in the captions, we have received considerable assistance from G. Croughton, J.R. Fairman, S. Hine, N. Langridge, D. Mason, R. Randell, E. Staff, N. Stanyon and R. Stevenson. We are very grateful for this assistance and for the endless help given by our wives.

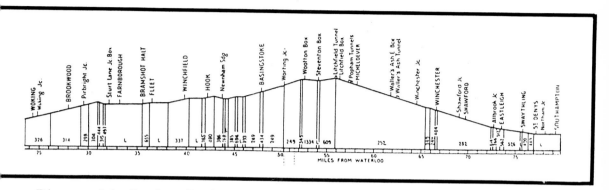

Diagram of the Southern Region in 1949, with Western Region routes shown with a narrow line.

All maps are to the scale of 25″ to 1 mile, unless otherwise stated.

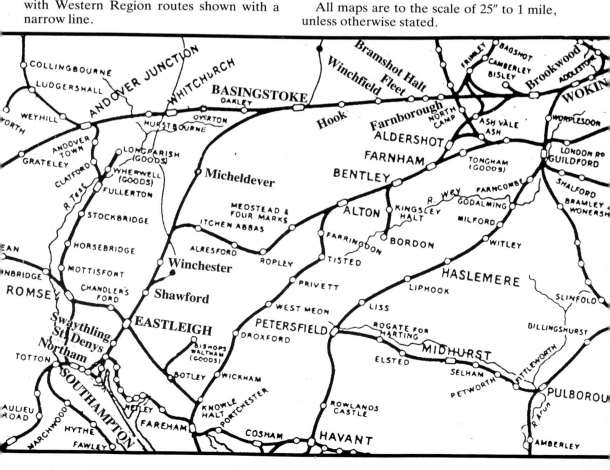

GEOGRAPHICAL SETTING

The route climbs steadily from the Bagshot Beds in the Woking area, onto the Bracklesham Beds around Brookwood and then onto another sandy deposit, the Barton Sands, in the vicinity of Pirbright Junction. The Blackwater River is crossed near Farnborough, from where the line traverses Bagshot Beds as far as Winchfield. The northward flowing River Whitewater is crossed between Winchfield and Hook, the route as far as the village of Basing being on London Clay. The Loddon Valley is crossed, east of Basingstoke.

For about 20 miles, the railway runs on Chalk formed by an eastward extension of Salisbury Plain. The Itchen Valley is entered near Winchester, this feature making an easy course for the railway constructors. The other geological feature of note is an area of Brickearth surrounding Eastleigh.

The geography of the Southampton district has given the city three important features which have helped to make it the ideal port. Firstly, the confluence of the Itchen and the Test give two adjacent water frontages. Secondly, the harbour is well sheltered and thirdly there are four high tides per day. This has for long been attributed to the presence of the Isle of Wight but recent studies have shown it to be associated with a mass of water that oscillates north-south, adding a "harmonic" component to the west-east twice daily sine wave of normal tides.

These important basic geographical facts caused the railway system to develop in this particular way.

HISTORICAL BACKGROUND

The London & Southampton Railway obtained its Act of Parliament in 1834 and opened the first section of its route from London (Nine Elms) to Woking Common on 21st May 1838. It was extended to Shapley Heath (now Winchfield) on 24th September of that year. The extension to Basingstoke and the Winchester to Southampton section came into use on 10th June 1839. The final part between Basingstoke and Winchester, with its numerous tunnels, was ready on 11th May 1840.

The London & South Western Railway had been formed in 1839 and opened its first branch from the route in 1841, to Gosport via Fareham, giving the Portsmouth area its first station.

The next branch was to a terminus at Guildford, coming into use on 5th May 1845. In 1847, a single line to Dorchester from Southampton Terminus was opened, via Ringwood. Also in 1847, the branch to Salisbury from Bishopstoke (now Eastleigh) commenced operation, via Romsey.

The LSWR monopoly of railway traffic at Basingstoke was lost in 1848, when the GWR opened a broad gauge branch from their main line at Reading.

The Basingstoke to Andover line was opened in 1854, the year in which a short branch from Brookwood to the nearby cemetery came into use.

1865 saw the alternative route from London to Winchester via Alton completed. Twenty years later, Winchester received a GWR operated line from Didcot and Newbury, which was not linked to the LSWR at Shawford Junction until 1st October 1891.

A branch from Portswood (now St. Denys) to Netley was opened in 1866.

A further branch at Brookwood came into use on 14th July 1890, running north to Bisley. The final link to the route was from Alton to Basingstoke, it being opened on 1st June 1901. The chequered history of this light railway is to be found in our *Branch Lines to Alton*.

Passenger services ceased to Brookwood Cemetery in 1941; to Bisley in 1952; to Newbury in 1960; to Romsey (from Eastleigh) in 1969 and to Alton (from Winchester) in 1973. Only the Romsey line now remains open for freight.

Electrification of the route from Woking to Pirbright Junction, for the Waterloo to Farnham trains, took place on 3rd January 1937, the full service to Alton starting on 4th July 1937. The conductor rail was extended to Bournemouth in 1967, with a partial service to Basingstoke commencing on 2nd January and to Bournemouth on 3rd April. The full electric timetable started in 1968.

PASSENGER SERVICES

The initial service to Basingstoke comprised six trains each way. By 1849, there were eight trains between Woking and Southampton, only one more being added by 1861. Only two or three tains ran on Sundays for most of the nineteenth century.

The 1890 timetable shows 11 main line trains calling at Winchester with 19 between London and Basingstoke. Twenty years later the figures were 20 and 26 respectively, the timetable showing no less than 38 stopping trains between Eastleigh and Southampton, on weekdays.

Through services between the GWR and Southampton, via their Didcot and Newbury route, started in 1891, with the LSWR hauling the trains south of Winchester until 1910. At about this time through services commenced between Bournemouth and the GWR via Basingstoke and Reading. The LNWR also started a through service to Bournemouth West from Manchester, via Willesden and Clapham Junctions.

Local passenger services were of lesser importance during the two World Wars. In WWI Southampton became the main port for movement of troops to and from France (mainly to, sadly). The vital role that the port (and the railways serving it) played during the invasion of Europe in WWII is not widely appreciated, but is graphically described in *War on the Line* (reprinted by Middleton Press).

Between the wars, the regular services were expanded and an increasing number of additional holiday trains provided. The latter reached a peak in the mid-1950s, with more inter-regional services provided than ever before.

Two named trains graced the line – the "Bournemouth Belle", which ran from 1931 to 1967 (apart from the years of war and austerity) and the "Royal Wessex", which was introduced in 1951. Certain boat trains also carried nameboards.

After decades of waiting, a completely revised regular interval electric service came into full operation in 1968, remaining basically unchanged for twenty years. Each hour, two stopping trains were provided between Woking and Basingstoke, one continuing all stations to Bournemouth. A semi-fast train called at Woking, Basingstoke, Winchester and Southampton Airport. Since 29th September 1986, the hourly non-stop Waterloo-Southampton trains have called at the airport station, then renamed Southampton Parkway.

Inter-regional services have seldom received names. Notable exceptions have included the "Pines Express", after it was diverted away from the Somerset & Dorset line in 1962, and the present "Wessex Scot". The decline and recent imaginative revival of these through services is illustrated below, the summer weekday frequency being shown (½ indicates a train divided in the north).

Destination	1938	1955	1964	1976	1987
Birkenhead	½	1			
Edinburgh	½				½
Glasgow	½				½
Liverpool				2	2
Manchester	½		1		2
Newcastle	1		1	1	1
York		1			

Boat trains were a feature of the route until recent times and a description of their diversity would occupy much more space than is available here. Train services between Woking and Brookwood and on the two branches from Brookwood will be mentioned in a future album, as will the Salisbury line services.

WOKING

1. Initially, the station had only one platform and was known as "Woking Common", the village being 1½ miles distant. Two platforms and a footbridge were soon provided. This view from the west end shows a train in the down loop, a feature that remained until the station was completely rebuilt in 1936-38. Bays on the up and down sides were also provided. (Lens of Sutton)

The Junction Box is shown at the divergence of the Portsmouth and Southampton lines, on the left of this 1913 edition. The Victoria Arch carries the road under twelve tracks, on the right. This page may be rolled slightly to link with the map of the station on the page after next.

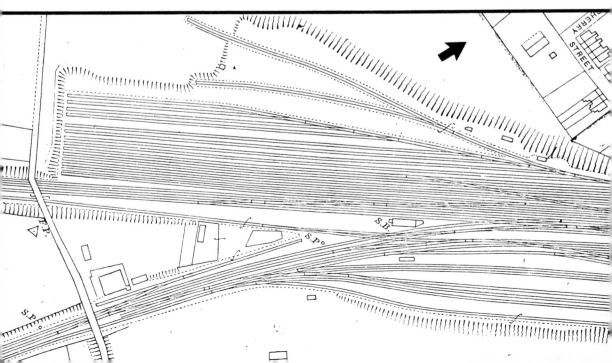

2. Until 27th June 1937, there were three signal boxes – East, Yard and Junction. Yard Box had 17 levers when erected in 1877 and backed onto the High Street – see S.B. on the map. Signalman Tom Matcham is on duty. (A.J. Simmonds)

←

3. The 1937 signal box was fitted with 131 miniature levers and continues in service over 50 years later. It is now bounded by much more modern panel boxes at Surbiton, Feltham, Basingstoke and Guildford. (British Rail)

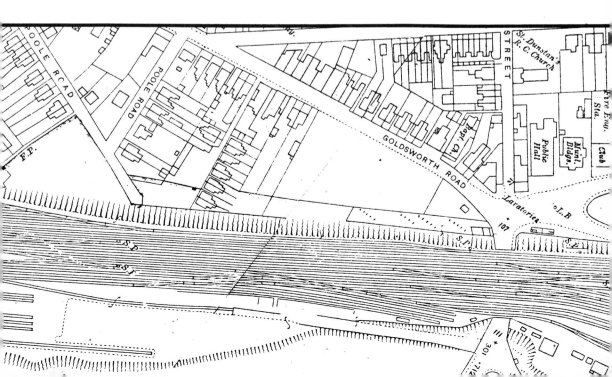

4. Looking west from the signal box in July 1955, we see the busy goods yard, which contained a 10-ton capacity crane. Less obvious is the junction for the Guildford line, which is just beyond the signals in the distance. Originally, the double track of the branch ran parallel to the main line, the junction being at the end of the platforms. (D. Cullum)

5. The signal box was regularly enveloped in exhaust from locomotives departing west from platform 4, as witnessed on 10th July 1966 as Merchant Navy class no.35010 *Blue Star* passes with the 10.30 Waterloo to Bournemouth service. (J.H. Bird)

6.   Some eyebrows were raised on 15th July 1966 when London Transport stock arrived in BR livery. The units were on crew training trips, prior to transfer to the Isle of Wight.

Other views of this station can be found in our _Waterloo to Woking_ and _Woking to Portsmouth_ albums and in Peter Hay's _Steaming through Surrey_.

The station was soon to become a busy interchange for road services to Heathrow Airport. (J.H. Bird)

The continuation of the 1913 map shows the 50ft. diameter locomotive turntable which was retained until electrification although the engine shed had closed in 1889 when the roundhouse at Guildford was opened. The station was officially "Woking Junction" from 1865 to 1918.

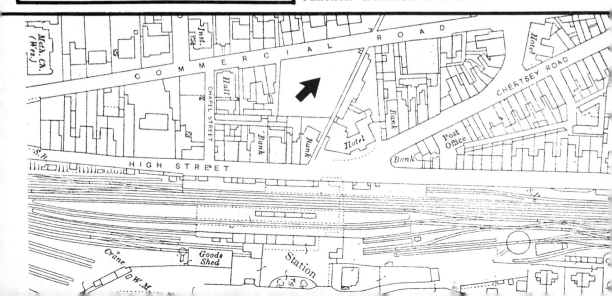

WEST OF WOKING

7. A West of England train is seen on the down main line, hauled by an Adams class T6 4–4–0, piloted by Drummond class L12 no.419. The down local is on the right and passes behind the Junction Box. This had been built in 1877 with 26 levers and was later fitted with a 100-lever frame in which 34 were unused upon closure in 1937. (Lens of Sutton)

8. 1967 was the last year of steam on the Southern Region and this route was the last steam operated main line in Britain. No.34089 *602 Squadron* had lost its nameplates when photographed on 3rd June of that historic year, hauling the 10.00 Waterloo to Exeter relief train. The previous photograph was taken from this bridge. (J.H. Bird)

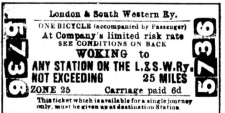

London & South Western Ry.
ONE BICYCLE (accompanied by Passenger)
At Company's limited risk rate
SEE CONDITIONS ON BACK
WOKING to
ANY STATION ON THE L.&S.W.Ry.
NOT EXCEEDING 25 MILES
ZONE 25 Carriage paid 6d
This ticket which is available for a single journey only, must be given up at destination Station

9. No.5578 roars west on 5th June 1970 and is viewed from the same bridge. By then, the former marshalling yard had been given over to permanent way materials, a use which still continues. Quadrupling of the tracks from here to Basingstoke was undertaken in 1901-04, although a third track to Pirbright Junction was in use by 1903. (J. Scrace)

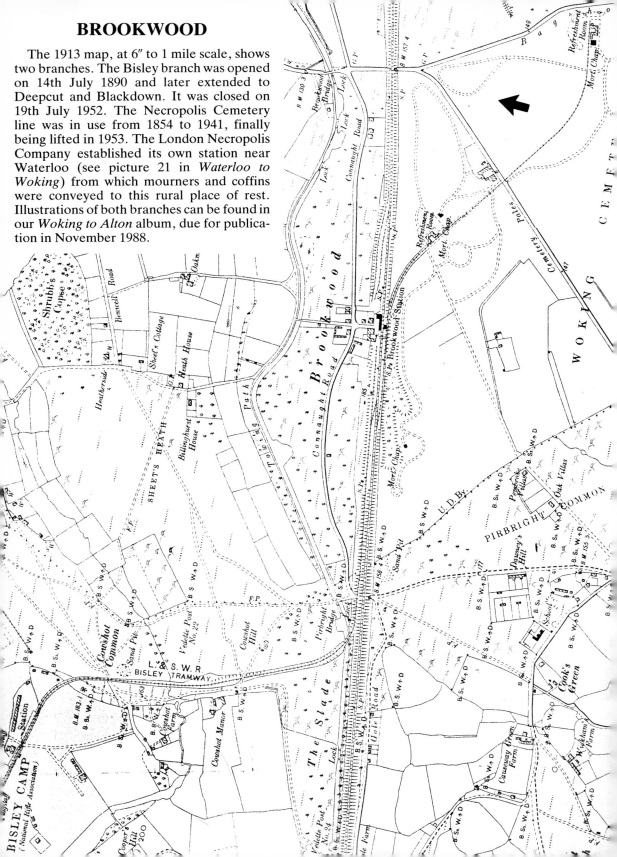

BROOKWOOD

The 1913 map, at 6″ to 1 mile scale, shows two branches. The Bisley branch was opened on 14th July 1890 and later extended to Deepcut and Blackdown. It was closed on 19th July 1952. The Necropolis Cemetery line was in use from 1854 to 1941, finally being lifted in 1953. The London Necropolis Company established its own station near Waterloo (see picture 21 in *Waterloo to Woking*) from which mourners and coffins were conveyed to this rural place of rest. Illustrations of both branches can be found in our *Woking to Alton* album, due for publication in November 1988.

10. There was little habitation in this area of poor agricultural land and so no station was provided when the line was built. A station was erected, at the expense of the London Necropolis Co. and opened on 1st June 1864, ten years *after* their branch line. This is the north elevation – the right hand part dating from 1890 and the remainder from 1903. (Lens of Sutton)

11. Ex-LBSCR class H2 4-4-2 *North Foreland* runs into the down platform which had been moved to its present position during the quadrupling work in 1903. The train is carrying visitors to the Farnborough Air Show on 7th July 1950 and is composed of borrowed ex-LNER air braked stock for which an ex-LBSCR engine was required. The goods shed was erected in 1903 and remained in use until 1966. (S.C. Nash)

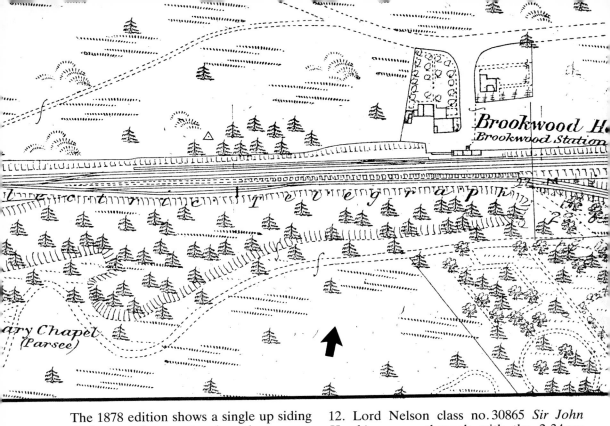

The 1878 edition shows a single up siding and a loop on the cemetery branch.

12. Lord Nelson class no. 30865 *Sir John Hawkins* races through with the 2.34 pm Waterloo to Bournemouth West service on 12th July 1952. The signal box was in use from July 1907 until 5th June 1966. Prior to 1904, there had been two boxes. (D. Cullum)

13. 1½ miles west of Brookwood, the junction for the Aldershot, Farnham and Alton line is reached, the route having run parallel to the Basingstoke Canal. A flyover for the up branch line was built in 1902 and is seen here in April 1963, just prior to the replacement of the steelwork by a series of concrete beams. The additional abutments are also evident. Conductor rails were laid as far as Sturt Lane Junction prior to the electrification of the Ascot-Aldershot services on 1st January 1939. (British Rail)

14. Not a scene on the Western Region but it is the approach to Deepcut on 16th October 1965, when D817 on a down Exeter train overtakes a Western DMU on a Woking-Basingstoke shuttle. The Warships were transferred in 1964-65 and the DMU shuttle started with the Summer timetable as steam was taken off the local services – indeed the non-commuter through services were themselves largely withdrawn. (G.P. Cooper)

15. Ex-LNER class A2 no.60532 *Blue Peter* passes through the 1½ mile long Deepcut cutting with a LCGB railtour to Exeter on 14th August 1966. The nearby village of Deepcut acquired its name from the canal or cut, which is up to 70ft. below ground level, in a cutting parallel to the railway. (G.P. Cooper)

16. At the west end of Deepcut cutting, the 1794 Basingstoke Canal crosses the railway. This is the scene on 24th July 1902, during the lengthening of the aqueduct to provide two more arches for the new tracks. It had been planned to avoid disruption of canal traffic. This photograph shows a wooden leat, hanging from a massive timber truss, carrying water from the stopped-off end of the navigation and indicates that the aim was not achieved. Pictures 30 to 33 in *Surrey Waterways* (Middleton Press) show other views of this interesting structure.

(P.A.L. Vine collection)

17. Sturt Lane Junction Box was on the south side of the main line and was in use from 1907 until 1966. The triangular junction with the line to Camberley and Ascot was taken out of use in October 1964. (D. Cullum)

The 1912 map at 6″ to 1 mile apparently shows a connection between the LSWR and SECR's Reading branch but the junction with the LSWR which, if completed, was never used regularly. The two signal boxes shown on the main line had in fact been replaced by the one illustrated, which was half way between its predecessors.

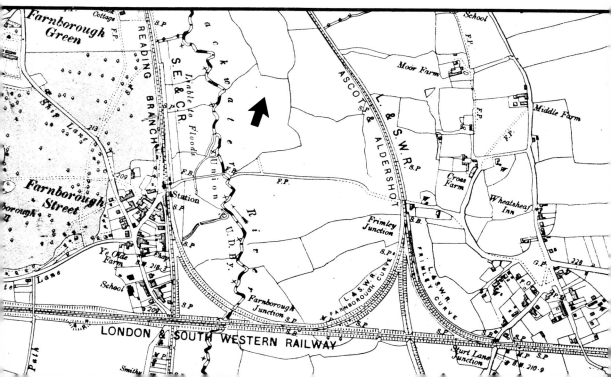

FARNBOROUGH

18. This photograph appears to have been taken before 1871, when a loop line was added behind the up platform. The colonnade, seen on the down platform, was smaller but similar to the one erected at the Gosport terminus. (D. Cullum collection)

The 1871 edition shows a plethora of wagon turntables but no signal box.

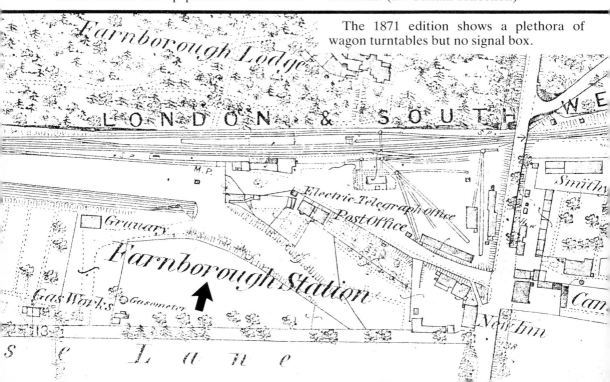

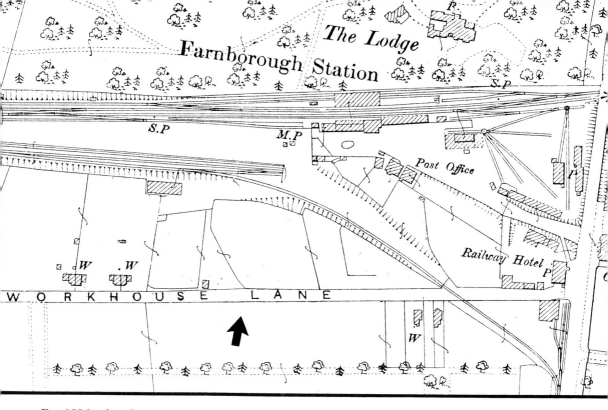

By 1896, the dangerous wagon crossing over the main lines had been removed and a signal box added at the east end of the down platform. The branch connected with the tracks of the Aldershot & Farnborough Tramways.

19. The cottage style design with dormer windows was chosen for the post-quadrupling station, harmonising well with its rural environment. Winchfield and Farnborough were initially the only intermediate stations between Woking and Basingstoke.
(D. Cullum collection)

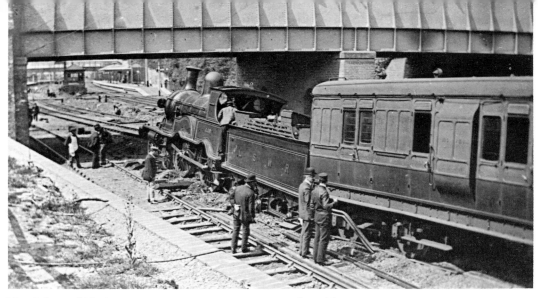

20. Adams 445 class no.448 appears to have run off temporary track during the widening work, in about 1904. The signal box was replaced by one at the west end of the down local platform on 28th May 1905. (Lens of Sutton)

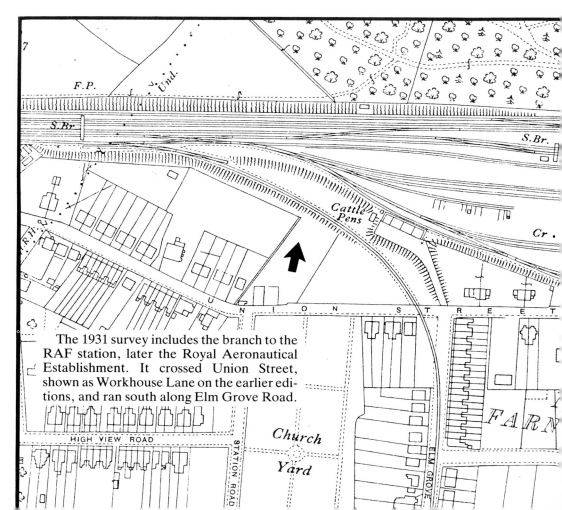

The 1931 survey includes the branch to the RAF station, later the Royal Aeronautical Establishment. It crossed Union Street, shown as Workhouse Lane on the earlier editions, and ran south along Elm Grove Road.

21. A Farnborough Air Display special passes under the A325 on 7th July 1950. K class no. 32348 hauls air braked Eastern Region stock, the ex-LBSCR engines being fitted with both air and vacuum brakes. Air Displays brought rich variety to the railway observers' notebooks and considerable revenue to BR. (S.C. Nash)

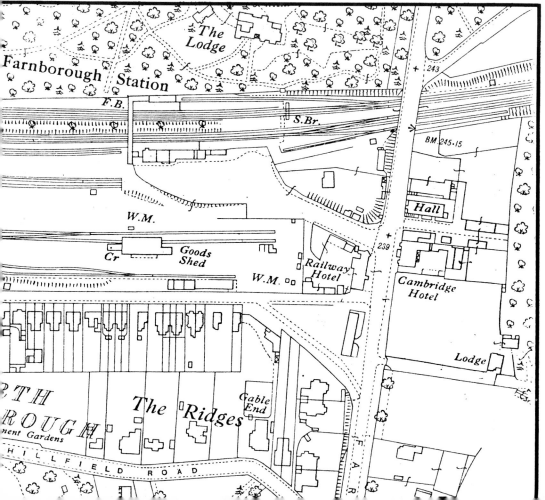

22. The island platform was little used and was given over to shrubs at an early date. This 1955 view shows that passengers then still had the luxury of a covered footbridge – now only the steps are roofed, despite a vast increase in London bound passengers. The coaches are standing at the military platform. (D. Cullum)

23. A westward view in 1955 shows the extent to which the new lines had to be curved. Air operated signals were in use between Brookwood and Basingstoke. Farnborough Box had 40 levers set at 3 in. centres instead of the 5 ins. required in mechanical frames. Intermediate signals were automatic – there were twelve between here and Fleet. (D. Cullum)

24. Merchant Navy class no.35023 *Holland-Afrika Line* rattles over the crossover and gives passengers their last opportunity to get smuts in their eyes on a Weymouth express. This is the 8.30 departure from Waterloo on Saturday 9th July 1967 – the last day of steam on the Southern Region and also a day for tears in many eyes. (G.P. Cooper)

25. The up bay platform lines and those from the down dock were removed in 1965 enabling both platforms to be lengthened to accommodate 12-car electric trains. D808 speeds towards Waterloo with the 7.25 from Exeter Central on 30th September 1969. (J. Scrace)

26. The last train from the RAE crosses Union Street on 10th April 1968. Coal for the boilers had been the main traffic but on that day there were also many passengers in the brake van, including a BBC film crew. The 1915 Hawthorn Leslie later went to the Isle of Wight Steam Railway where it hauls passengers regularly. (G.P. Cooper)

The terminal layout of the RAF branch, as shown on the 1931 edition.

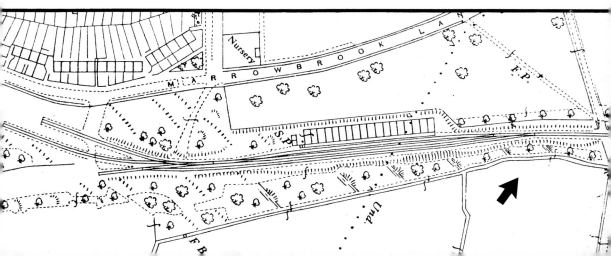

BRAMSHOT HALT

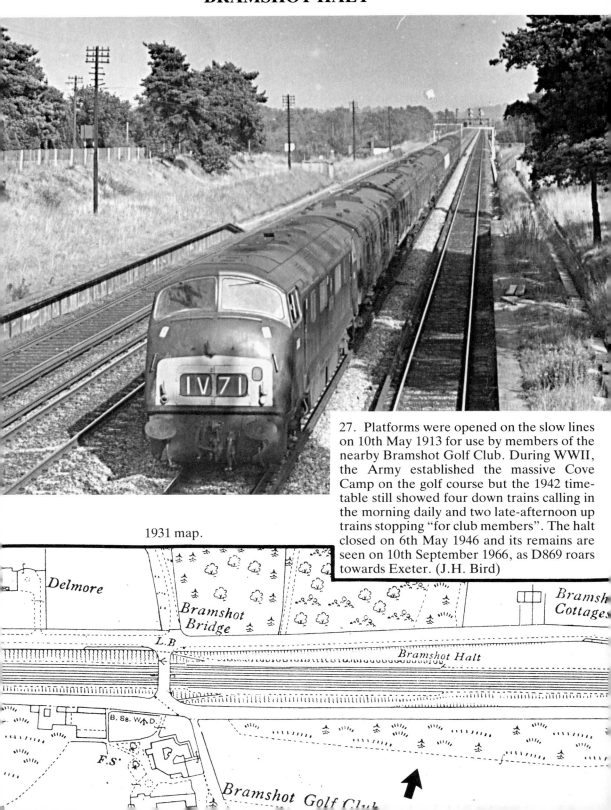

27. Platforms were opened on the slow lines on 10th May 1913 for use by members of the nearby Bramshot Golf Club. During WWII, the Army established the massive Cove Camp on the golf course but the 1942 timetable still showed four down trains calling in the morning daily and two late-afternoon up trains stopping "for club members". The halt closed on 6th May 1946 and its remains are seen on 10th September 1966, as D869 roars towards Exeter. (J.H. Bird)

1931 map.

FLEET

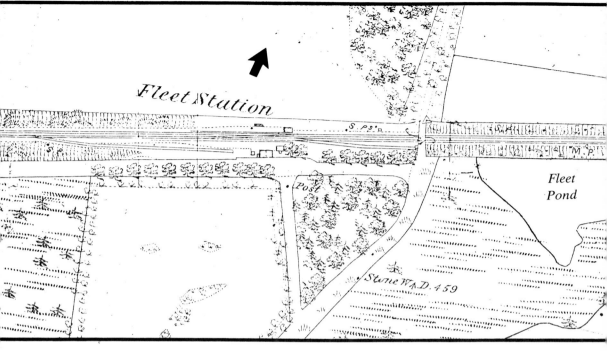

The 1871 edition shows that the first station, which opened in 1847, was on the west side of the road and that there were no houses in the vicinity.

28. At the quadrupling in 1904, a new station was built on the east side of the highway and, logically, no island platform was provided for the fast lines. This postcard view is towards London, from the down platform.
(Lens of Sutton)

29. The carriage canopy or porte cochère added to the architectural features on the down side, but the ventilator above the gentlemens toilets was very indiscreet – the Victorian era had passed.
(D. Cullum collection)

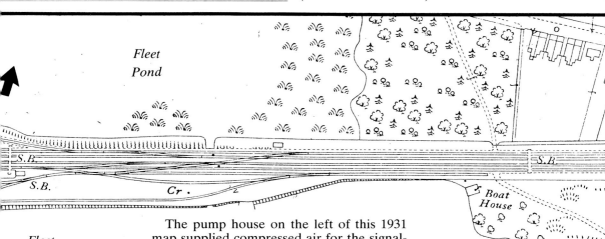

Fleet Pond

Fleet Pond

The pump house on the left of this 1931 map supplied compressed air for the signalling system. The steam engine was replaced by an electric motor in 1958.

30. The goods shed, on the left, was erected on land reclaimed from Fleet Pond. The station was named after this notable geographical feature until 1869. (Lens of Sutton)

31. No. 418 was a class L12 but as the tender is much smarter than the locomotive maybe the engine bore a different number. This 1939 photograph shows the Basingstoke to Farnborough pick-up goods, the brake van of which is close to the signal pump house.
(D.H. Wakely/
J.R.W. Kirkby Collection)

32. In 1966, the station was demolished and replaced by unphotogenic flat-roofed "CLASP" buildings. The photographer avoids including these on 20th March 1987, as no. 50043 *Eagle* speeds past with the 5.48 from Exeter, displaying logos for the myopic. (J.S. Petley)

WINCHFIELD

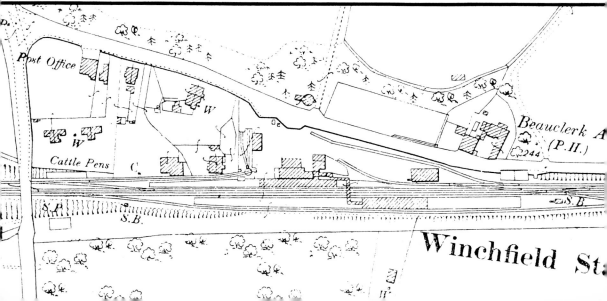

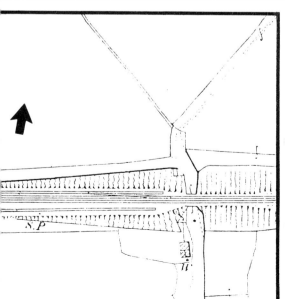

33. Opened as Shapley Heath, the tiny country station was the terminus from 24th September 1838 until 10th June 1839. This is the view from the road bridge, looking towards Woking soon after the 1904 quadrupling. The goods yard is on the right but the 4-ton crane is on the left.
(D. Cullum Collection)

The 1896 survey reveals the position of the two signal boxes and that all goods facilities were then on the north side of the line.

34. The two earlier signal boxes were replaced by this air operated one on 25th September 1904, which was photographed in 1911 with Signalman Arthur Dunford on duty. It remained in use until 30th October 1966 and had 48 levers of which 12 were spare. They controlled 34 signals and 28 points, as each lever had more than one operating position.
(A.J. Simmonds Collection)

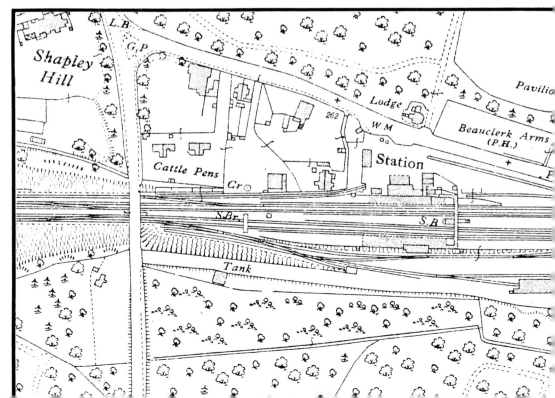

35. The prestigious "Bournemouth Belle" passes the entrance to the goods yard on the 14th July 1962, hauled by no. 34010 *Sidmouth*, devoid of the headboard. The signal bridge has two walkways for the lampman – one at the base of the ladders and the other for the coacting lower arms. (S.C. Nash)

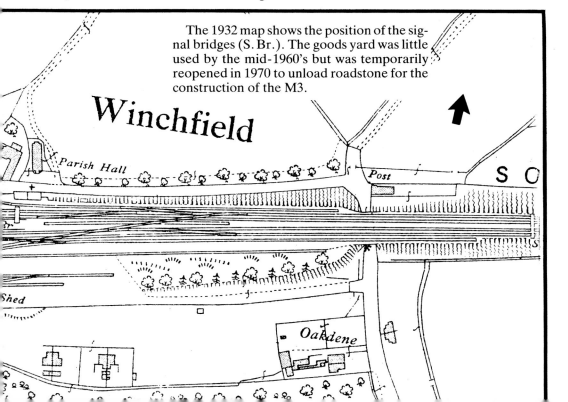

The 1932 map shows the position of the signal bridges (S. Br.). The goods yard was little used by the mid-1960's but was temporarily reopened in 1970 to unload roadstone for the construction of the M3.

Winchfield

Parish Hall

Post

S O

Shed

Oakdene

36. As at Farnborough, the down lines deviate from the straight owing to the earlier presence of an island platform. Here, and at Hook, the buildings and curved platform canopy were retained on the up side after the quadrupling. A 4TC set from Salisbury is hauled towards Waterloo on 5th October 1985 by a class 33/0, no. 33023. Normally class 33/1s are used on this service, as they are capable of push-pull operation. (J.S. Petley)

SOUTHERN RAILWAY.

Cunard White Star Ltd. R. M. S." Queen Mary"

Southampton Docks to

(211) (No.1)   (No.1) (211)

WATERLOO

EXCESS TOURIST TO ORDINARY

Issued in conjunction with First Class
Tourist Ticket No.

First Class.   Fare 5/5

0000   0000

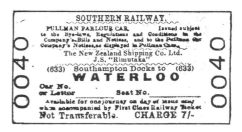

SOUTHERN RAILWAY.

PULLMAN PARLOUR CAR.   Issued subject
to the Bye-laws, Regulations and Conditions in the
Company's Bills and Notices, and to the Pullman Car
Company's Notices, as displayed in Pullman Cars.
The New Zealand Shipping Co. Ltd.
J.S. "Rimutaka"
(633) Southampton Docks to (633)

WATERLOO

Car No.
or Letter   Seat No.

Available for one journey on day of issue only
when accompanied by First Class Railway Ticket
Not Transferable.   CHARGE 7/-

0040   0040

37. Winchfield cutting, west of the station, has presented slippage problems, despite its small angle of repose. Clay has spread out over the down local line in this undated eastward photograph, taken from the site of the present M3 overbridge. Beyond Hook, the clay was of benefit to the railway in that it provided traffic at the private siding of the Danes Hill Brick & Tile Works. (British Rail)

HOOK

38. The station opened on 2nd July 1873 and the down side was rebuilt, as seen, in 1904. Note that the new island platform was not hard paved and that the footbridge was not glazed. Some economies were made during the expensive quadrupling. (Lens of Sutton)

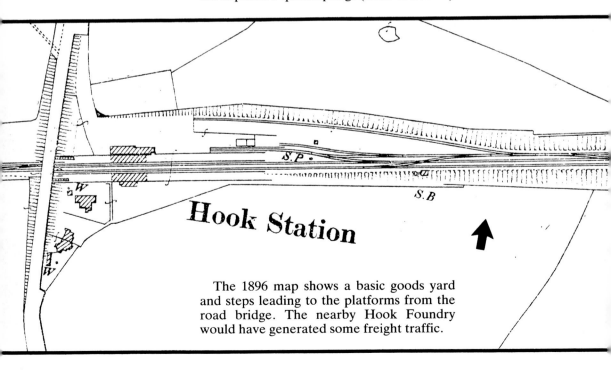

Hook Station

The 1896 map shows a basic goods yard and steps leading to the platforms from the road bridge. The nearby Hook Foundry would have generated some freight traffic.

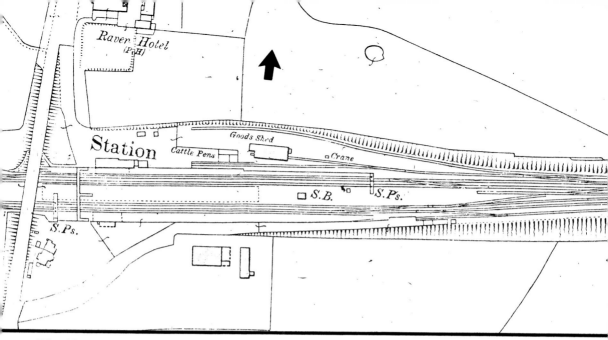

The 1911 survey reveals that little changed in the goods yard after quadrupling, except that a goods shed was erected. The crane could lift 5 tons.

39. An air cylinder stands by the 40-lever box. Pressure was low – only 15 psi, with the machines working at only half that. This is the scene on 1st July 1963 as an up express speeds past the grass mound that was once the island platform. (H.C. Casserley)

40. The simple up side building is similar to the one still retained at Winchfield. Both were still in use in 1988 serving a much larger number of travellers than their builders could have envisaged. The goods yards at all the intermediate stations have been converted to car parks. (C. Hall)

1856

DOWN PASSENGER TRAINS ON THE MAIN LINE. LONDON TO SOUTHAMPTON.

Distance from London.	STATIONS.	DAILY. 1	2	3	4	5	6	7	8	9	10	11	12	13	DAILY. 14	15	16	17	18	19	20	21	22	23	24	25	26	27
		Hampton Court.	Southampton.	Parly. to Southampton.	Hampton Court.	Alton.	Weybridge.	*Southampton.	Hapmton Court	Exp. Southampton.	Necropolis.	Hampton Court	Alton.	*Southampton.	Hampton Court.	Godalming.	Exp. Southampton.	Hampton Court.	*Southampton.	Hampton Court.	*Southampton.	W king.	Hampton Court.	Woking.	Alton.	Hampton Court.	*Southampton.	Hampton Court.
Miles.	LEAVE	a.m.	a.m.	a.m.	a.m.	a.m.	a.m.	a.m.	a.m.	a.m.	a.m.	a.m.	p.m.	p.m.	p.m.	p.m.	p.m.	p.m.	p.m.	p.m.	p.m.	p.m.	p.m.	p.m.	p.m.	p.m.	p.m.	p.m.
	WATERLOO BR.	6 45	7 0	7 15	9 5	9 40	9 55	10 15	10 30	11 0	11 20	11 30	12 30	1 0	2 0	2 20	3 0	3 30	4 0	4 30	5 0	5 10	5 50	6 10	7 0	8 10	8 30	10 45
1¼	Vauxhall	6 51	....	7 25	9 11	9 46	....	....	10 36	....	....	11 36	12 36	....	2 6	2 26	....	3 36	....	4 36	....	....	5 56	....	7 6	8 16	....	10 51
4½	Clapham	7 0	..	7 37	..	9 55	..	..	..	..	..	11 45	12 45	..	2 15	..	..	3 45	..	4 45	..	..	6 5	..	7 15	8 25	..	11 0
7¼	Wimbledon	7 8	....	7 48	9 23	10 3	....	....	10 48	....	....	11 53	12 53	....	2 23	....	....	3 53	....	4 53	....	....	6 11	....	7 23	8 33	....	11 8
9¾	Malden	..	..	7 57	..	..	..	....	..	..	..	12 0	..	..	2 30	..	..	..	..	5 0	..	..	6 20	..	7 30	8 40	..	11 15
12	Kingston	7 20	7 25	8 5	9 35	10 15	...	10 39	11 0	11 21	....	12 6	1 5	*	2 38	2 50	3 21	4 5	4 25	5 6	5 24	5 33	6 26	6 33	7 38	8 46	8 55	11 22
14½	Esher	..	7 32	8 15	..	10 23	..	..	..	..	..	..	1 12	..	..	2 57	..	..	4 32	..	..	5 40	.	6 40	7 45	..	9 3	..
17	Walton	....	7 39	8 24	....	10 30	....	....	....	....	....	....	1 19	....	....	3 4	....	....	4 39	....	....	5 47	....	6 47	7 53	....	*	....
19	Weybridge	..	7 47	8 34	..	10 36	10 40	10 53	..	11 32	..	..	1 26	1 36	..	3 11	3 32	..	4 46	..	5 36	5 54	..	6 54	8 0	..	9 15	..
24¼	Woking	....	8 0	8 55	....	10 50	....	11 3	....	11 40	....	....	1 38	1 47	....	3 21	3 40	....	4 58	....	5 40	6 7	....	7 7	8 15	....	9 28	....
	Necropolis Junction	..	..	..	..	..	..	..	..	..	12 20	..	..	..	..	..	..	..	..	..	..	..	..	..	..	..	..	..
33	Farnborough	....	8 20	9 27	....	....	....	11 20	....	....	....	....	....	2 10	....	....	....	....	5 18	....	5 55	....	....	....	....	....	9 48	....
36½	Fleetpond	..	..	9 37	..	..	...	..	..	..	..	..	..	..	..	..	..	..	*	..	..	..	..	..	..	..	..	..
39	Winchfield	....	8 34	9 48	....	....	....	11 35	....	....	....	....	....	2 25	....	....	....	....	5 33	....	6 10	....	....	....	....	....	10 2	....
47¾	Basingstoke	..	8 50	10 15	..	..	..	11 55	..	12 15	..	..	..	2 45	..	..	4 15	..	5 50	..	6 28	..	..	..	..	..	10 18	..
58	Micheldever	....	9 12	10 50	....	....	....	12 20	....	....	....	....	....	3 10	....	....	....	....	6 12	....	*	....	....	....	....	....	10 40	....
66½	Winchester	..	9 26	11 10	..	..	....	12 37	..	12 50	..	..	..	3 28	..	..	4 50	..	6 28	..	7 5	..	..	..	..	..	10 56	..
73¼	Bishopstoke	....	9 45	11 32	....	....	...	12 52	....	1 5	...	....	....	3 45	....	....	5 5	....	6 47	....	7 20	....	....	....	....	....	11 15	....
78¾	SOUTHAMPTON	..	9 57	11 47	..	..	..	1 7	..	1 17	..	..	..	3 57	..	..	5 17	..	6 59	..	7 35	..	..	..	..	..	11 27	..

* No. 7. Train stops at Esher and Weybridge on Saturdays.
No. 13. Train will stop at Kingston by Signal to take up only.
No. 18. Train will stop at Fleetpond to set down London Passengers when required.
No. 20. Train will stop at Micheldever on Mondays to set down London Passengers when required.
No. 26. Train will stop at Walton to set down London Passengers when required.

41. A view from the road bridge on 18th March 1987 shows a class 73/1 hauling the 06.11 service from Weymouth, composed of two 4TC trailer sets. The leading one, unusually, includes a buffet car which was removed from one of the 4REP powered sets. The 4REPs were withdrawn so that their motors could be reused in the replacement Wessex Electrics planned for the Weymouth services from May 1988. (J.S. Petley)

The 1911 edition includes the Dane Hill Brick & Tile Works, which was 1½ miles west of Hook. The siding was in use until 1964 and was controlled by Newnham Box until 1902 – thereafter by a ground frame.

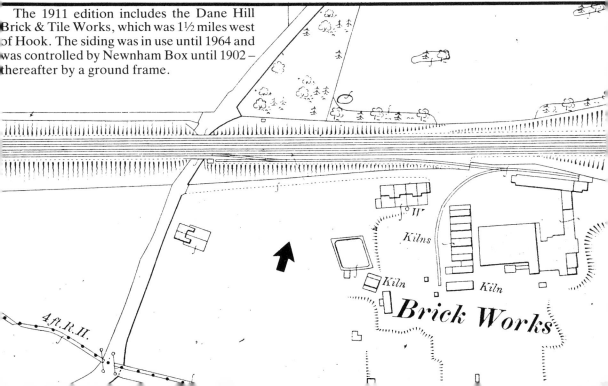

BASINGSTOKE

42. The first station had a small building, on the down side, similar in design to the present Micheldever premises and was on a site at the London end of the present up platform. On the left is the second LSWR station, which was completed by 1851, and on the right we see the GWR terminus, opened in 1848. (Lens of Sutton)

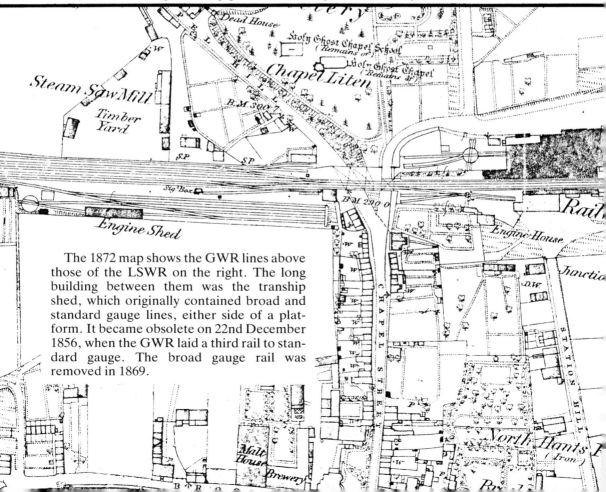

The 1872 map shows the GWR lines above those of the LSWR on the right. The long building between them was the tranship shed, which originally contained broad and standard gauge lines, either side of a platform. It became obsolete on 22nd December 1856, when the GWR laid a third rail to standard gauge. The broad gauge rail was removed in 1869.

43. In about 1875, the bridge over Chapel Street was widened to take four tracks and the platforms were extended over it. Its girders are seen in the foreground after the station was rebuilt with four through platforms, in about 1903. The work took 2½ years to complete and included two new goods yards (west of the station), a bigger goods shed and a 3-road engine shed. (Lens of Sutton)

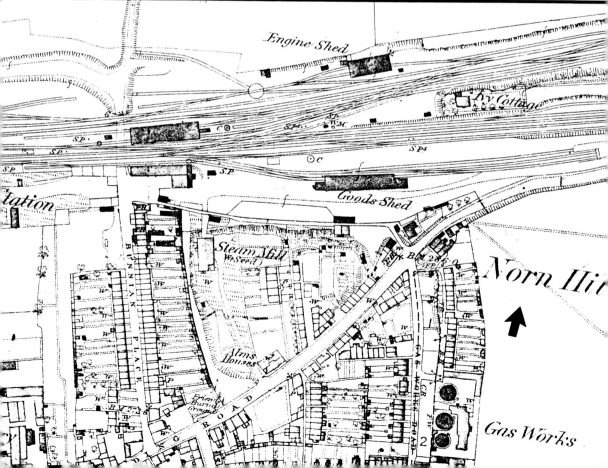

44. This is the south elevation of the town's third LSWR station and, like its predecessors, was situated on the downside. Unlike the earlier two, it had a subway for passengers and luggage. The station served a population of about 8000 in 1891; 17,000 in 1951 and 75,000 in 1981. Traffic has grown accordingly – over 2¼ million passengers now travelling annually! (Lens of Sutton)

45. A down train departs on 7th July 1926, behind one of Drummond's class S11, no. 404, built at the same time as the station, in 1903. The massive goods shed, of similar date, is on the right, in the down yard. (H.C. Casserley)

46. Class X6 no. E663 obscures the connection to the GWR in July 1929, although part of the GWR yard is visible. At this time the SR used the prefix E to refer to engines of Eastleigh or LSWR origin. Basingstoke East Box is visible. It was redesignated "A Box" on 27th May 1956 and closed on 20th November 1966. (Dr. I.C. Allen)

47. A July 1929 photograph shows that railings still separated the two stations. GWR trains continued to use their own platforms until 1st January 1932 when they transferred to the SR up bay, platform 5. A Reading bound service stands in platform 4, behind class T3 no. 560. (Dr. I.C. Allen)

49. A 3-coach set was sufficient for the 11.12 stopping service to Waterloo on 2nd May 1962. No. 34041 *Wilton* is standing on the points leading to the Reading line, which had become part of the Southern Region (to Southcote Junction) in 1950. (J. Scrace)

48. An undated photograph taken from a down train during the transition from gas to electric lighting reveals an arch in the end of the GWR station. Reference to the map shows that a line once passed through it to a turntable – later a connection to the LSWR up goods yard was laid through it. It was known as "No. 6 road". (Lens of Sutton)

50. The 1904 three-road locomotive shed was near the west end of platform 4 and ceased to be a running shed in 1963 although it remained as a signing-on point until the end of steam. A 70ft turntable was brought from Burnaby Road, near Portsmouth Harbour, in 1942 and an electric coaling crane was installed in 1943. Both are behind the camera in this July 1964 view. The tall chimney is on the sand drier. (E. Wilmshurst)

52. The all electric box came into use on 20th November 1966, controlling the main line between the Farnborough and Micheldever areas. Ex-Metropolitan Railway no. 12 *Sarah Siddons* was photographed on 20th September 1985. The next day she worked a rail-tour of Kent – see the last picture in our *Ashford to Dover* album. (J. Scrace)

51. The new signal box frame was complete when photographed on 27th September 1965. The former GWR box is visible on the left and the five Barton Mills carriage sidings commence under the Reading Road bridge, on the right. These were reduced to four and lengthened upon electrification. (British Rail)

Rain Gauge.

Pumping Station
(ingstoke Corporation)

Tank

Public
ming Bath

King George's
Playing Field

Mission
Hall

The 1932 edition shows that at the west end of the up yard a branch curved away northwards. It commenced with a loop and then climbed at 1 in 53 for about one mile to Park Prewett Hospital. It was in use from 1914 until 1950. Official closure was on 21st May 1954 and lifting took place in 1956. On the south side of the main line, the Basingstoke & Alton Light Railway diverged. The sidings shown were for Thorneycroft's lorry factory. This eventually expanded on the other side of the branch and an additional siding was provided to the new works. Illustrations of this branch and other views of Basingstoke station are to be found in our *Branch Lines to Alton*.

W.M.

Motor Works

Football
ound

Tennis
ounds

Saxon Burial
ound

SOUTH OF BASINGSTOKE

53. 1½ miles west of Basingstoke, the route begins to turn south, near Winklebury. A troop special from Farnborough to Yeovil enters the gentle curve on 17th June 1959, hauled by two T9s, nos. 30338 and 30718. (S.C. Nash)

54. 2½ miles from Basingstoke, the Salisbury and Southampton lines diverge, at Worting Junction. BR class 5 no. 73116 *Iseult* has run down the incline from Battledown Flyover and is crossing to the up fast line, with a Bournemouth to Waterloo train. (E. Wilmshurst)

55. Battledown Flyover and quadruple track between it and Basingstoke came into use on 30th May 1897, many years before quadrupling to London was completed. SR class N15 no. 786 crosses over the Salisbury lines, the junction signal box for which stood close to the camera, before the flyover was built. The remains of its successor are seen near the rear of the train. (Dr. I.C. Allen)

57. Having passed through the 198 yd. long Litchfield Tunnel, no. 34025 *Whimple* tears towards the Popham Tunnels (265 and 199 yds.), one mile north of Micheldever. It is hauling the down "Bournemouth Belle" on Monday 3rd July 1967, the beginning of the last week of main line steam in Britain. (G.P. Cooper)

56. "West Country" class *Clovelly* rumbles over the span, on 7th July 1967, just two days before the official end of steam operation. It was hauling the empty stock of an earlier boat train. Southwards, intermediate signal boxes were provided at Wootton, Steventon, Waltham and Litchfield, until 1966. In the 1930s, there were two sidings for Steventon Manor, on the up side near Waltham Box. (G.P. Cooper)

58. A landslide immobilised 4VEP no. 7754 when running up from Micheldever on 26th January 1985. No. 33104 was sent "wrong road" to the rescue but collided with it in darkness. No. 33023, the next rescue engine, has separated the victims, while the Eastleigh breakdown crane waits in attendance. (J.H. Bird)

MICHELDEVER

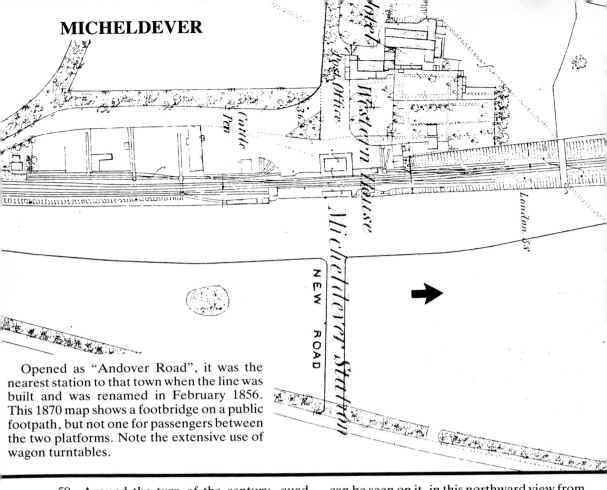

Opened as "Andover Road", it was the nearest station to that town when the line was built and was renamed in February 1856. This 1870 map shows a footbridge on a public footpath, but not one for passengers between the two platforms. Note the extensive use of wagon turntables.

59. Around the turn of the century, quadruple track was laid through the station and an island platform provided. The signal box can be seen on it, in this northward view from the loading dock. (Lens of Sutton)

60. Chalk being an ideal material for civil engineering structures, LSWR developed a massive quarry at this location. It is viewed across the north end of two loops. In the early 1930s, chalk was removed at the rate of 5000 tons per week in connection with the construction of the new docks at Southampton. (Lens of Sutton)

61. Unquestionably the most appealing architecture on the route, the station was constructed of local flint with attractive yellow brick quoins. The all round verandah gives additional charm. The poster in this WWII view asks "is your journey really necessary?" (F.E. Box/NRM)

MICHELDEVER

62. The island platform became disused as fast trains sped through non-stop but in 1966 the loop lines were removed and the island restored to regular use by the hourly stopping train service to Bournemouth. The signal box closed on 13th November 1966. (J. Scrace)

The 1910 edition shows a few of the quarry sidings. Eventually there were over 20 sidings, many of which were used for storage of stock awaiting repair or scrapping at

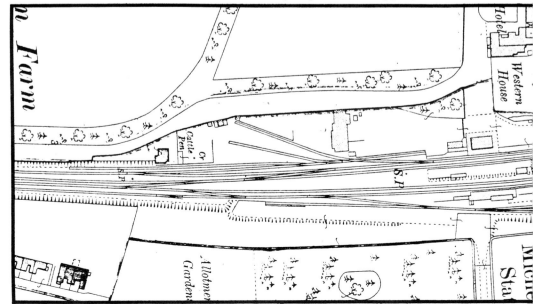

63. The 13.30 Waterloo to Weymouth train speeds south behind no. 34017 *Blandford Forum* on 15th August 1966, four months after the loops had been removed. In 1988, only a few of the sidings remained in use, holding tankers. These brought petroleum products in (to the Elf terminal) and took crude oil away from the wells of the nearby Larkwhistle Farm oilfield. (J. Scrace)

Eastleigh. Every imaginable commodity was stored there prior to D-Day, the location thus becoming known as "Woolworths".

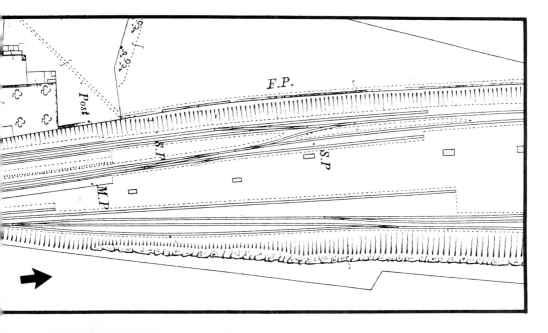

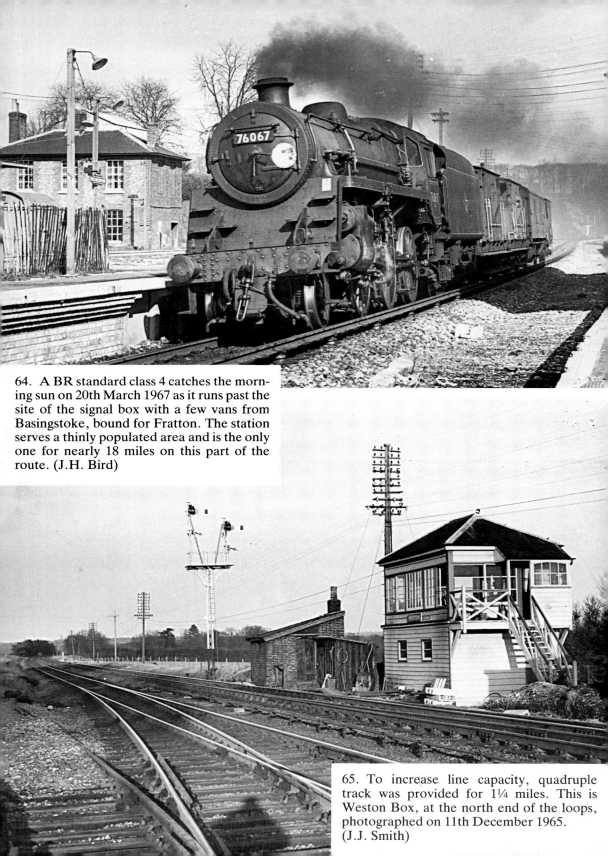

64. A BR standard class 4 catches the morning sun on 20th March 1967 as it runs past the site of the signal box with a few vans from Basingstoke, bound for Fratton. The station serves a thinly populated area and is the only one for nearly 18 miles on this part of the route. (J.H. Bird)

65. To increase line capacity, quadruple track was provided for 1¼ miles. This is Weston Box, at the north end of the loops, photographed on 11th December 1965. (J.J. Smith)

66. Another northward view shows Wallers Ash Box, at the South end of the loops, on the same day. The relatively flat nature of the chalk plain is evident, although the route climbs at 1 in 252 for nearly 10 miles. Much sweat was lost by firemen of up trains in this region. Wallers Ash tunnel (501 yds) is to the south. (J.J. Smith)

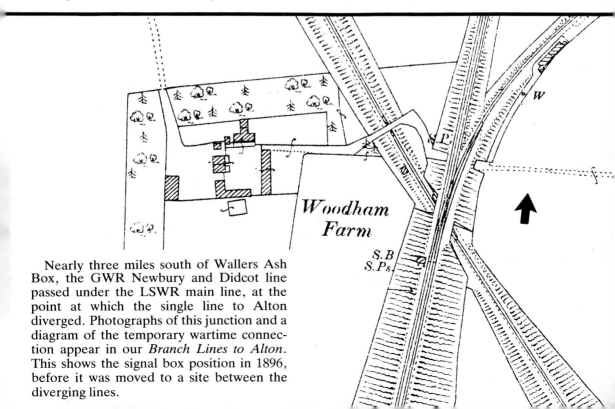

Nearly three miles south of Wallers Ash Box, the GWR Newbury and Didcot line passed under the LSWR main line, at the point at which the single line to Alton diverged. Photographs of this junction and a diagram of the temporary wartime connection appear in our *Branch Lines to Alton*. This shows the signal box position in 1896, before it was moved to a site between the diverging lines.

WINCHESTER

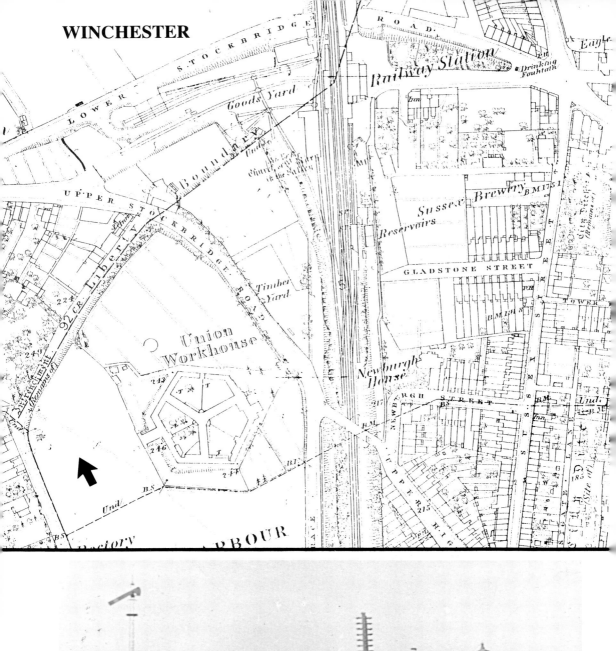

The 1871 survey reveals a plethora of wagon turntables and a long shed covering the down siding. This was probably for carriages, as a goods shed is shown on the up side.

67. The name "Winchester City" was applied by BR between 26th September 1949 and 10th July 1967, to avoid confusion with the former GWR "Chesil" station. Class X2 no. 583 arrives with a down train and almost obscures the signal box.

← (E.R. Lacey Collection)

68. A photograph taken from the Upper Stockbridge Road Bridge in 1925 shows a substantial chimney which is thought to have been part of the pumphouse associated with the reservoirs shown on the maps. Locomotive water supplies were obtained from them. (P. Rutherford)

69. The goods shed wall forms part of the support for the up platform canopy. The goods yard closed on 6th January 1969, nine years after this photograph was taken. In 1988, the shed was largely used for servicing motor cars. (H.C. Casserley)

The 1897 edition shows that sharp curves resulted from the abolition of the turntables and that an additional yard had been developed north of the station.

70. Because of the sharp curves, shunting of the yard was restricted to the short wheelbase 0-4-0 B4 class for many years. The corrugated iron clad shed, on the left, was provided in about 1928, for the shelter of the engine on weekdays. It returned to Eastleigh at weekends. The shed was erected immediately north of St. Paul's Church, the southern part of the triangular layout having been removed. The photograph was taken on 20th September 1962. (J. Scrace)

71. In 1965, the southern connection to the goods yard was removed to allow for the extension of the down platform. This shows progress on 25th May, as class N no. 31873 passes with a down van train. (J. Scrace)

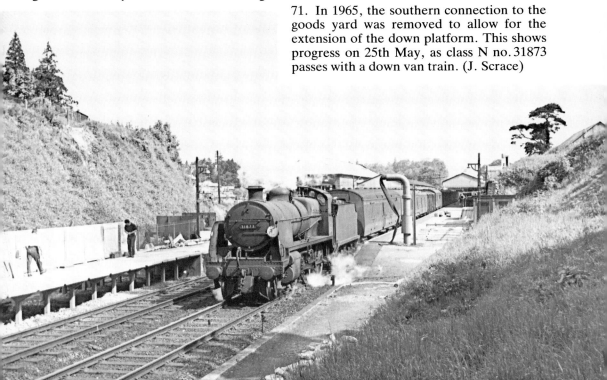

72. Dieselisation of many local Hampshire services took place in 1957-59. DEMU no. 1123, bound for Eastleigh, arrives on 29th May 1966. The signal box came into use on 13th November 1960 and was closed exactly six years later. It was still standing in 1988, in use as a permanent way office. (C.L. Caddy)

London and South Western Railway.

The *First Class Train* will perform the journey in three hours, taking *First Class Passengers only*, excepting that accommodation will be afforded for a limited number of Servants in Livery. The Fare will be **20s.** each Passenger; the Fare for Servants in Livery **13s.** each. This Train will not call at any Stations between London and Woking Common, but will take up and set down Passengers at all the Stations between Woking Common and Southampton.

The Fare from London to Southampton by the *Mixed Trains* will be **18s.** First Class; **12s.** Second Class.

The *Third Class* Passengers will be taken by the Day Goods Train only.

The *Mail Trains* call at Kingston, Weybridge, Woking Common, and all Stations to the West of Woking Common. The Fares the same as the Mixed Trains for both First and Second Class Passengers.

OMNIBUSES convey Passengers to and from the Station near Vauxhall, from the following Coach Offices, viz.—the Spread Eagle, Gracechurch-street; Swan with two Necks, Lad-lane; Cross Keys, Wood-street, Cheapside; White Horse, Fetter-lane; George and Blue Boar, Holborn; Golden Cross, Charing-cross; and Universal Office, Regent-circus.—Fare 8d.

STEAM BOATS convey Passengers to and from the Railroad, from and to Old Swan Pier, Old Shades Pier, Upper Thames-street, Hungerford Market, Waterloo and Westminster Bridges, at 4d.

POST HORSES are kept at the Station, and Carriages are taken to, or fetched from, any part of London, at a charge of 10s. 6d. including the driver.

Passengers.   Horses and Carriages.

Distance	STATIONS.	FAST TR. 1st Class.	MIXED TRAIN. 1st Class.	MIXED TRAIN. 2nd Class.	GOODS TR. 3rd Class.	CARRIAGE	1 HORSE.	2 HORSES.	3 HORSES.
Miles.		s. d.	s. d.	s. d.	s. d.	s. d.	s. d.	s. d.	s. d.
3	London to Wandsworth	..	1 0	0 6	..		not taken		
6	.... Wimbledon	..	1 6	1 0	..		not taken		
10	.... Kingston	..	2 0	1 6	..	10 0	7 0	10 0	12 0
13	.... Esher and Hampton Court	..	2 6	1 6	..	10 0	7 0	10 0	12 0
15½	.... Walton	..	3 0	2 0	..		not taken		
17½	.. Weybridge	..	3 6	2 0	..	10 0	7 0	10 0	12 0
23	.... Woking	6 0	5 0	3 6	2 6	12 0	8 0	12 0	15 0
31½	.... Farnborough	8 6	7 6	5 0	3 0	17 0	11 0	17 0	21 0
38	.... Winchfield	10 0	9 0	6 0	3 6	21 0	14 0	21 0	26 0
46	.... Basingstoke	12 0	11 0	7 0	4 0	26 0	18 0	25 0	30 0
56	.... Andover Road	15 0	13 6	9 0	5 0	31 0	22 0	30 0	36 0
64	.... Winchester	17 6	15 6	10 0	6 0	36 0	25 0	34 0	42 0
76¾	.... Southampton	20 0	18 0	12 0	7 0	42 0	30 0	40 0	50 0

73. BR class 4 4–6–0 no. 75069 displays its double chimney on 27th August 1966, in the days when parcel traffic justified regular van trains of this length. Both platforms had been lengthened and conductor rails were in position, ready for the greatest change the line had ever witnessed. (D. Fereday Glenn)

74. 4 VEP unit no. 7774 forms part of the up semi-fast service to Waterloo on 4th July 1987. The single remaining siding is electrified and in 1988 was used only by the 6.10 departure for Bournemouth, on weekdays. In 1918, a military platform was provided on this line, which was then a loop. It was known as the Baltic siding, owing to the timber traffic once handled. (J. Scrace)

75. 1¼ miles south of Winchester, the line passed over a minor level crossing near St. Cross. *Woolacombe* is seen with the up "Pines Express" in 1965 close to St. Cross Box which ceased to be used in 1969 when the crossing was closed to the public. (J.H. Bird)

SHAWFORD JUNCTION

76. The junction with the GWR route was ¾ mile north of the station and the line as far as Chesil (originally Cheese Hill) station was owned and maintained by the LSWR. A down express approaches the junction box, the Didcot line being just visible behind it. (Lens of Sutton)

77. The Gainsborough Model Railway Society had the use of Alan Pegler's *Flying Scotsman* on 18th May 1963 for an excursion from Lincoln to Southampton. The white posts on the right are for the single line tokens. The line in the foreground was added in March 1943, as a relief line for the additional traffic to the docks. (E. Wilmshurst)

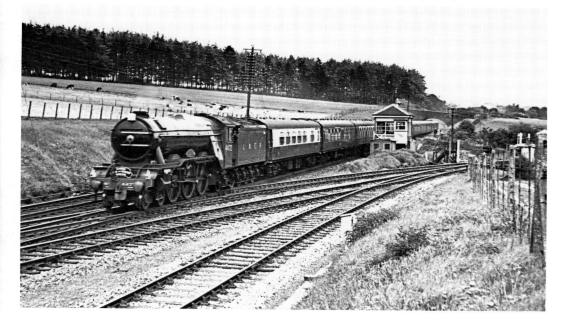

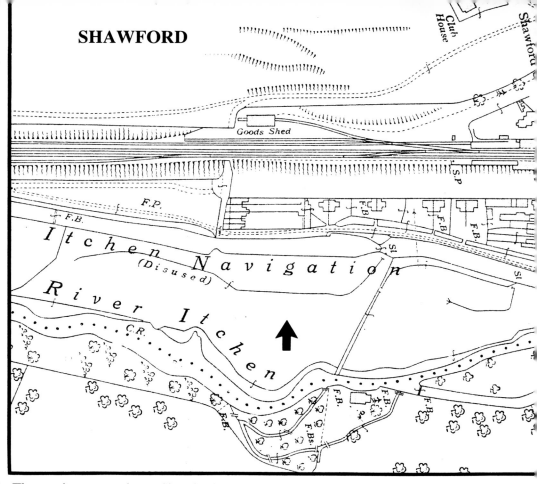

SHAWFORD

Goods Shed

Itchen Navigation (Disused)

River Itchen

78. The station opened as "Shawford and Twyford" on 1st September 1882. Here we see a down Western Region train from Didcot running on the 1943 relief line which connected with the 1931 down local line, just south of the station. Regular services via Winchester Chesil ceased on 7th March 1960 although a few local trains from Southampton terminated there on summer Saturdays until September 1961. (Lens of Sutton)

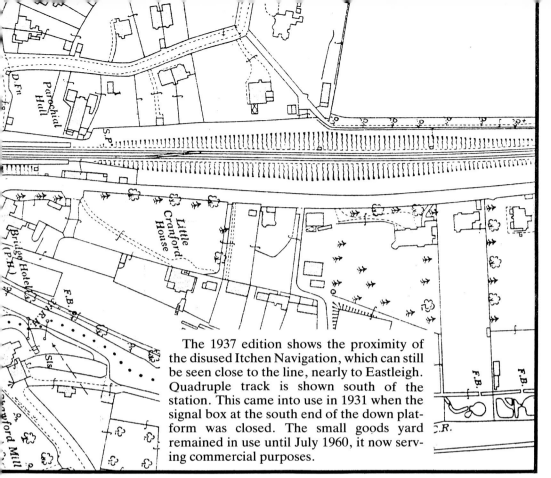

The 1937 edition shows the proximity of the disused Itchen Navigation, which can still be seen close to the line, nearly to Eastleigh. Quadruple track is shown south of the station. This came into use in 1931 when the signal box at the south end of the down platform was closed. The small goods yard remained in use until July 1960, it now serving commercial purposes.

79. On the right of this May 1966 northward view are the new concrete fencing panels at the back of the relief line platform and the railings of the footway linking it to the barrow crossing. Passenger access to both down platforms is by steps up from the road. The station offices are at road level, on the up side, but both the canopies have now gone. (C.L. Caddy)

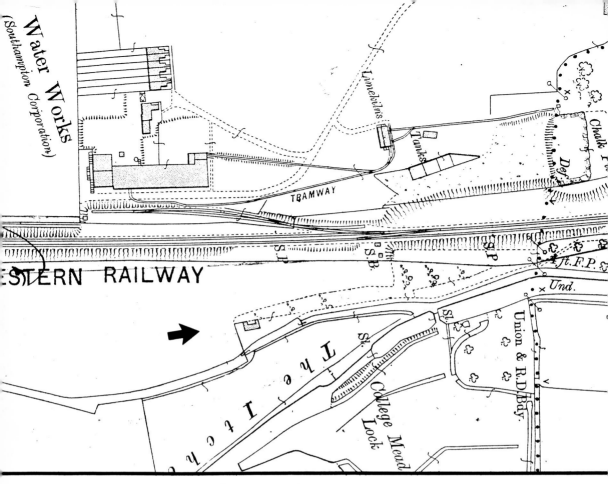

The 1909 survey shows the waterworks siding, which remained usable until 1969. It was located one mile south of Shawford. The nearby signal box was named Otterbourne and was replaced by a ground frame in 1931.

80. Class M7 no. 30128 approaches Eastleigh East Yard on 25th June 1950 with the 12.05 Alton to Southampton service. In the background is Allbrook Junction Box, which remained in use until 1966, and in the foreground is the No. 1 Up Goods line, which was removed in the same year. (D. Cullum)

EASTLEIGH

The 1864 edition of the 1″ to 1 mile survey reveals the remoteness of the first station from habitation and the reason why it was named "Bishopstoke", a name it retained until becoming "Eastleigh and Bishopstoke" on 1st July 1889. On the left is Chandlers Ford, on the Salisbury branch, and at the bottom is Swaythling, before it acquired a "y" and a station.

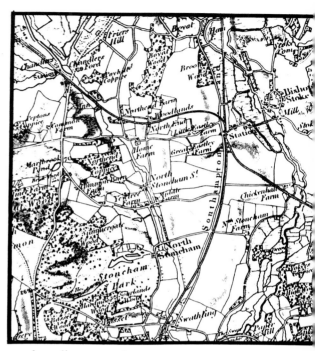

81.   The addition of an up loop line necessitated the provision of a new entrance and footbridge. This remains in use today, the booking office being located on the upper floor of the original building, which is retained on the island platform.
(Lens of Sutton)

82. The original station, with its coupled chimneys, became largely obscured by other buildings and platform canopies, and remains so today. Fenestrated chimney stacks were to be found on the contemporary stations at Gosport, Fareham and Southampton Terminus. (Lens of Sutton)

Noteworthy features of the 1886 map are the small dimensions of the engine shed and turntable; the presence of a large cheese market but few houses. The Gosport line is lower left and the Salisbury line is upper right.

83. Eastleigh East Box is to be seen in this and the previous photograph. North Box was on the Salisbury line and is just off the 1886 map. The former closed in 1966 and the latter in 1917. Class X2 no. 594 arrives with a down train from Waterloo to Southampton Terminus on 8th September 1931. (D. Cullum collection)

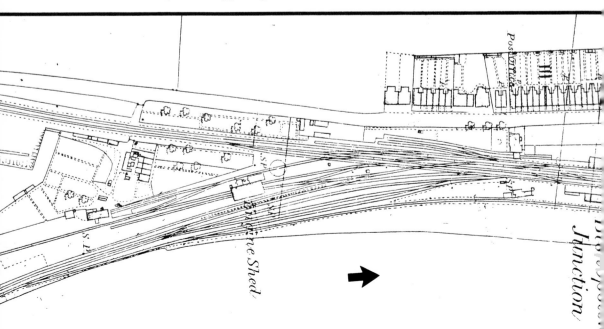

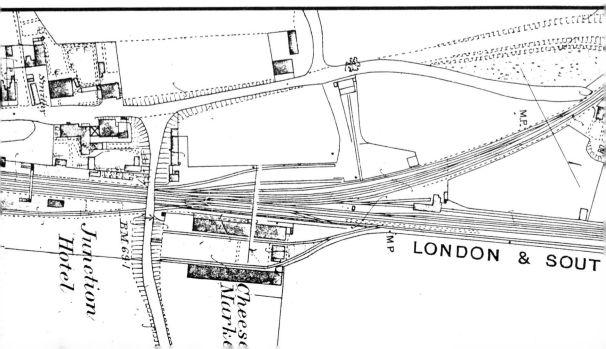

Junction Hotel

BM 69.1

Cheese Market

M.P.

M.P.

LONDON & SOUT

84. A rare wartime photograph shows a serviceman's "Boat Train" from Southampton, prior to attachment to a Bournemouth West to Waterloo service on 23rd March 1940. The locomotive is class X6 no. 658.
(D.H. Wakely/J.R.W. Kirkby collection)

The LSWR erected a new carriage and wagon works in 1891, part of it showing on this 1896 map. Extensive housing development took place at this time to accommodate the workers. The up loop line and a larger goods yard were also added, together with the marshalling yard, on the left.

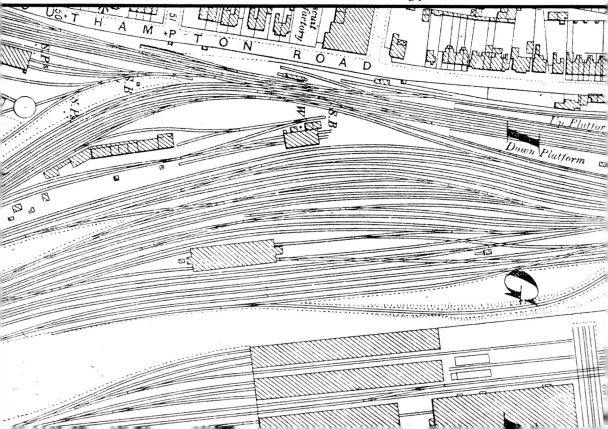

85. A view of the south end of the station looking north on 5th July 1945 includes a Didcot to Southampton train, complete with a clerestory coach. Beyond the trees are the lines to the locomotive works and to Fareham. (H.C. Casserley)

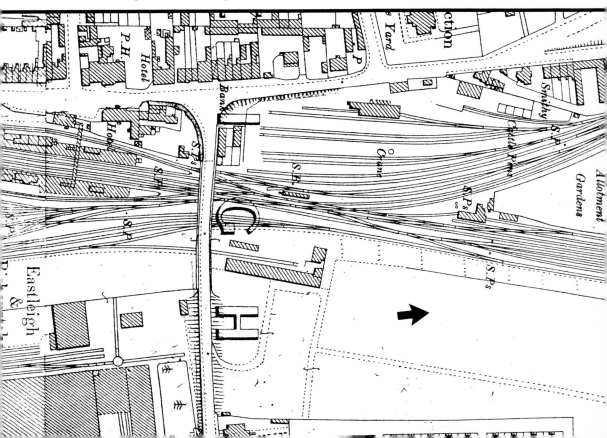

86. The 7.20 Liverpool to Poole service takes the through road on 30th June 1976, headed by no. 47101. The Romsey and Salisbury line curves away behind the leading coach and the 1966 signal box is behind the third one. The siding for Travis & Arnold's timber yard closed in 1965 and had been beyond the rear coach. (J. Scrace)

87. Looking north from the up platform in 1976, we see the concrete slab building which was added to the architectural jumble in 1967. It housed train crew quarters, offices and a buffet. The electrified up loop line was taken out of use on 4th January 1981. (J. Scrace)

88. Another architectural oddity is the cut back canopy on platform 4, the brackets of which project forlornly. No. 45032 leaves the yard in April 1985, many sidings having been subsequently removed. The locomotive works is in the background. (D.J. Kemp)

THE PINES EXPRESS

RESTAURANT CAR EXPRESS

BETWEEN

MANCHESTER, LIVERPOOL, WOLVERHAMPTON, BIRMINGHAM,

AND

SOUTHAMPTON CENTRAL, BOURNEMOUTH
VIA OXFORD AND BASINGSTOKE

From NORTH to SOUTH—WEEK DAYS ONLY		From SOUTH to NORTH—WEEK DAYS ONLY	
	am		am
Manchester (Piccadilly) ... . dep	10 0	Bournemouth West .. .. dep	10 0
Stockport (Edgeley) .... "	10 11	Bournemouth Central .... "	10.10
Liverpool (Lime Street) .. .. "	9 45	West Cowes Pier .. .. dep	9 5
Crewe .... "	10 55	Southampton Central .... dep	10 46
Shrewsbury .. .. "	11 35	Winchester City.. .. .. 1.. .. "	11 9
Wellington .. .. "	11 50	Basingstoke .. .. "	11 40
	pm		pm
Wolverhampton (Low Level) .. .. "	12 20	Reading West .. .. arr	12 3
Birmingham (Snow Hill) .. .. "	12 43	Oxford .... "	12 48
Leamington Spa General .. .. "	1 8	Banbury .. .. "	1 25
Oxford.... .. .. "	2 4	Leamington Spa General .. .. "	1 50
Reading West .. .. "	2 45	Birmingham (Snow Hill) .. .. "	2 23
Basingstoke .. .. arr	3 8	Wolverhampton (Low Level) .. .. "	2 47
Winchester City.. .. .. "	3 34	Wellington .. .. "	3 12
Southampton Central .... "	3 52	Shrewsbury .. .. "	3 26
West Cowes Pier .. .. arr	6 10	Crewe .. .. "	4 11
Bournemouth Central .... "	4 32	Hartford .. .. "	4 41
Bournemouth West .. .. "	4 44	Runcorn .. .. "	4 55
		Liverpool (Lime Street) .. .. "	5 18
		Wilmslow .. .. "	4 45
		Stockport (Edgeley) .... "	4 58
		Manchester (Piccadilly) .. .. "	5 9

89. The original station is picked out in white and the former swinging luggage platform is visible under the footbridge in this May 1981 picture. Beyond the road bridge is East Yard, which had three reception roads, two up goods roads and over 20 sidings. In 1988, special facilities were in use for an ICI methanol terminal and for loading Ford Transit vans, while many sidings are used by engineers' trains. (J. Scrace)

90. Turning the camera about 90°, we see the extent of the locomotive works and no. 73101 hauling the 15.45 Northam to Northfleet train of empty cement tanks. A single reversible line is provided for the first ½ mile of the route to Fareham. It is seen curving away, behind the fourth bogie. (J. Scrace)

EASTLEIGH WORKS

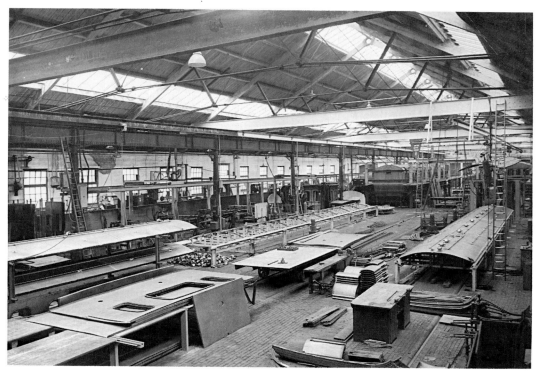

91. The Carriage & Wagon Works was established in 1891 and closed in 1968, although carriage repair has continued in the nearby former locomotive works. This undated photograph was marked "new steel carriage – general view of jigs for roof assembly". "New" presumably refers to the design. (British Rail)

92. The locomotive works transferred from Nine Elms in 1909 and was in production until 1965. Since then it has only undertaken repairs. This is the view of the dump in 1949, and it also shows the south side of the Works. (Lens of Sutton)

93. Open Days bring much pleasure to modern traction enthusiasts and benefit to railway charities. This is the scene in the former erecting shop on 12th October 1986 when nos. 33107, 33064, 33117, 73107 and 73111 were under repair. (D.J. Kemp)

EASTLEIGH SHED

94. The first and second sheds are shown in the top left corners of the two maps of Eastleigh. The third and much larger shed came into use in 1903 and was provided with this coaling stage. It was double sided and had three more columns on the other side. Class X6 no. 666 is seen on 12th September 1936. (H.C. Casserley)

95. This is the south end of the 15-road shed, which remained in use until the end of steam, having an allocation of up to 120 engines at its zenith. On the right of this May 1962 view is the 20,000 gallon water tank – workshops were provided on the left. (J. Scrace)

96. A southward view from the bridge to the works (seen on the right of picture no.90) shows the main line in the centre, the double track to the locomotive shed on the left and the Dorset siding on the right. Beyond it, in this 1966 view, is the grass covered connection to the four Stoneham sidings. These were added in 1943 and were in use until 1951. They were reopened temporarily in 1965-66. (D. Cullum)

97. A diesel depot was built to the east of the locomotive shed and is seen in the course of extension in February 1959. The houses on the right separate it from the locomotive works, the coaling stage being on the left. There is access to this depot from the Fareham line, which results in tracks completely encircling the works. (British Rail)

98. Standing outside the extended depot on 9th April 1981 is no. 47143, alongside the latest in suburban rolling stock. Despite great standardisation on BR, Eastleigh still offers the railway observer a very varied visual diet. (J. Scrace)

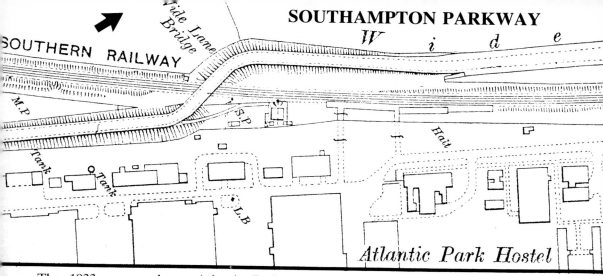

Atlantic Park Hostel

The 1933 survey shows Atlantic Park Hostel and a halt with a platform on the down line only. The hostel was established by a group of shipping lines and was used by emigrants prior to departure from Southampton Docks. The buildings had mostly been erected during WWI, for the US Naval Air Station. Passengers arrived from the north and departed southwards, so that only a down platform was needed. It was officially opened on 30th October 1929 and was in use for about five years, which included a period of great depression. Wide Lane Bridge replaced a level crossing and was brought into use in May 1907. Emigrants' final journey on British soil was usually made in a train of four or five elderly compartment coaches.

99. Commercial flying at Southampton Airport developed after WWII, with regular services to the Channel Islands. In 1987, there were 15 flights per day. A down local service passes through the station shortly before it was opened on 1st April 1966. After full electric services were introduced, it was served by the hourly semi-fast service. The former crossing keeper's cottage is on the right. (J.H. Bird)

100. On 5th October 1987, the name was changed from South-ampton Airport to South-ampton Parkway and al-most all trains were booked to call. This north-ward view in August 1987 shows the new up platform building and some of the 330 car parking spaces. (J. Scrace)

SWAYTHLING

101. The district began to develop as a high-class outer suburb of Southampton and so a station was opened on 15th October 1883. This helped it to grow further and, in 1930, it became the last district to be connected to the electric tramways. A public footpath runs between the station and the goods yard – the end of the middle siding is on the extreme right. (Lens of Sutton)

102. Another view from the footbridge reveals the extent to which the LSWR carriage designers felt the need to ventilate the compartments. The nearest coach has no less than six lavatories. The competing trams made inroads into traffic receipts and lasted until 1949. (Lens of Sutton)

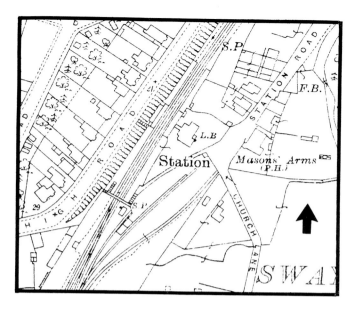

The 1933 map includes the small goods
yard and the cattle pens near the footbridge.

103. The exterior has a number of architectural features similar to contemporary stations at Brookwood, Shawford, Swanwick and Worplesdon. In 1988, it continued to fulfil its original function and had changed little since this photograph was taken in 1963. During WWII, an unexploded bomb in the booking hall necessitated closure of the down line for several days. (C.L. Caddy)

104. The Poole to York train heads north on 29th June 1966, behind ex-LMS class 5 no. 45145. The signal box closed five months later, the goods yard (which had been opposite it) having been closed in 1956 and lifted in 1961. (J.H. Bird)

105. A Waterloo to Weymouth service speeds south, through the well kept station, on 15th August 1987. The station is the nearest one to Southampton University and to the Ford Motor Company's Transit factory. (J. Scrace)

ST. DENYS

106. The first platforms were north of the present ones, close to the St. Denys Road bridge, and came into use on 1st May 1861. The branch to Netley was opened on 5th March 1866 when the station was moved to its present site. It was known as "Portswood" until 1876. (Lens of Sutton)

107. The previous picture was taken from the bridge seen in the background of this May 1952 view. The locomotive is class M7 no. 30029 and the train is a down local from Eastleigh. Quadruple track to Northam was brought into use on 4th May 1902. (H.C. Casserley)

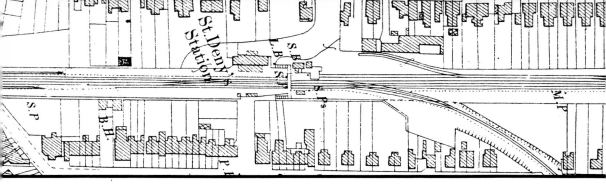

The 1897 map shows the single line to Fareham branching off, north of the station. The signal box, located on the up platform, closed in 1899.

The 1933 map includes the additional platforms which were provided in 1899, when the junction was rearranged.

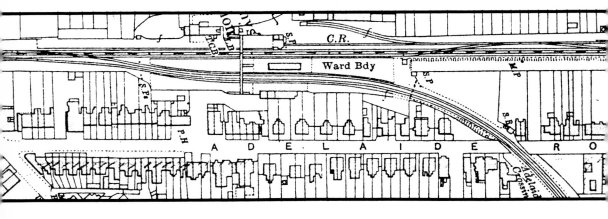

108. The Italianate style building survived in 1988, being similar in style to its contemporary at Netley. Unusually, the canopy does not reach the platform edge. Ex-LMS class 5 no. 45493 runs through platform 2, with an inter-regional service in 1966. (J.H. Bird)

109. This signal box was opened in 1899 and closed on 11th October 1981. Dukes Road level crossing was situated here until 1902. The shut off road can be seen in picture no.106. This photograph was taken in July 1966. (J.J. Smith)

110. Looking south from Dukes Road bridge, again in 1966, the broad expanse of the River Itchen at high tide comes into view. On the right are the Bevois Park sidings (pronounced Bevis), which were opened in 1901. Many of the 24 tracks were lifted in 1969 but lines were retained for Cadbury Schweppes (on the right), MAT Cartrain (centre) and Rugby Tunnel Cement on the left. (D. Cullum)

111. Despite most of the level crossings on the route having been steadily eliminated, Mount Pleasant crossing remains in use today, albeit operated under CCTV from Eastleigh Box. This 1966 view of the beautifully balanced rail-built up signal gantry includes the massive electrically operated gates, which were replaced by full lifting barriers in July 1967. (J.J. Smith)

The 1910 map shows Northam Junction in the top left corner, with the station nearby. Further south is Southampton Junction, initially the only junction, the spur to permit direct running from London to Bournemouth being opened in July 1858. The line to Belvidere Wharf later served Corrall's Dibles Wharf. This continued to carry coal traffic until July 1987, since when local coal distribution has been centred at Totton. The Chapel Tramway (lower right) became steam operated in 1902 and closed in 1967.

112. On the east side of the quadruple track a 15-road locomotive shed was in use, until replaced by the new one at Eastleigh in 1903. The site was used for two reception roads and the twelve Mudford's sidings, one of which led to the Itchen Wharves, near the present TVS Studios. The signal box controlled the southern entry to the yard and the junction of the lines to the Terminus and Central stations. It replaced one on the other side of the main lines in 1923 and was taken out of use on 11th October 1981. (J.J. Smith)

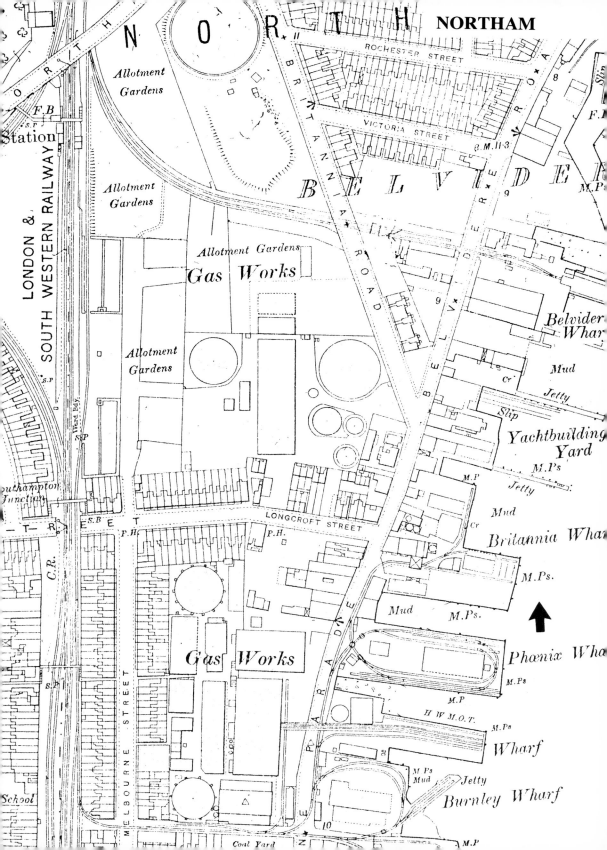

113. Looking north, Northam Junction is visible just beyond the bridge, on which the station offices are situated. The station was opened on 1st December 1872 and closed on 5th September 1966. (Lens of Sutton)

114. A Royal Train hauled by no. E6009 approaches Southampton Junction in 1969. The curve to the Central station, on left, ceased to be used on 9th December 1973 and the down line to the docks was removed in 1980. The goods line, on the right, was added in about 1900 and later doubled. (J.H. Bird)

SOUTHAMPTON TERMINUS

115. The imposing east facade of the original station is seen in 1939, with part of the train shed roof visible on the right. The frontage of the original London terminus, at Nine Elms, was similarly recessed behind five taller arches. "Southampton Town and Dock" station was the name that was used from 1896 until 1912. It became "Southampton Town for Docks" until being renamed "Terminus" on 9th July 1923. Note the street tramway terminus outside the hotel. (F.E. Box/NRM)

116. In 1928 a glazed roof was erected over the roadway between the end of the six platforms and the South Western Hotel. Many readers will remember that metal nameplate embossing machines were also to be found on many other stations. (Lens of Sutton)

117. Until about 1910, LSWR engines hauled most GWR trains south of Winchester Chesil. Thereafter locomotive variety increased at the terminus – an example is "Duke" class no. 3280, shown in about 1935. The South Western Hotel, in the background, has more recently accommodated Radio Solent and BBC TV studios. (C.R.L. Coles)

118. Southampton Yard Box was located on the south side of Central Bridge, which was nowhere near Central Station. The box remained in use until 13th December 1970, although regular passenger services ended on 5th September 1966. (J.J. Smith)

119. Class 4 2–6–0 no. 76061 bears a small headboard proclaiming that it is the last steam train to leave the station. It is hauling the 16.02 to Bournemouth on 3rd September 1966. The diesel is standing on one of the two lines to the Western Docks. Trains crossed Canute Road under the protection of a hand-held red flag. (J.H. Bird)

120. Part of the station was reopened for parcel and mail traffic from November 1966 until March 1968. No. D2083 is seen on 18th November 1967, when part of the former railway hotel was used as offices by Cunard. (J.H. Bird)

The still busy Southampton Central is illustrated in our *Southampton to Bournemouth* album and other views and maps of the St. Denys to Southampton Terminus section are to be found in our *Portsmouth to Southampton* volume. Photographs of many of the stations on the route are included in Peter Hay's *Steaming through East Hants*.

MP Middleton Press

Easebourne Lane, Midhurst, West Sussex, GU29 9AZ
☎ Midhurst (073 081) 3169

BRANCH LINES
BRANCH LINES TO MIDHURST
BRANCH LINES TO HORSHAM
BRANCH LINES TO EAST GRINSTEAD
BRANCH LINES TO ALTON
BRANCH LINE TO HAYLING
BRANCH LINE TO SOUTHWOLD
BRANCH LINE TO TENTERDEN
BRANCH LINES TO NEWPORT
BRANCH LINES TO TUNBRIDGE WELLS
BRANCH LINE TO SWANAGE
BRANCH LINES TO LONGMOOR
BRANCH LINES TO LYME REGIS
BRANCH LINES **AROUND** MIDHURST
BRANCH LINE TO FAIRFORD

SOUTH COAST RAILWAYS
BRIGHTON TO WORTHING
WORTHING TO CHICHESTER
CHICHESTER TO PORTSMOUTH
BRIGHTON TO EASTBOURNE
RYDE TO VENTNOR
EASTBOURNE TO HASTINGS
PORTSMOUTH TO SOUTHAMPTON
HASTINGS TO ASHFORD*
SOUTHAMPTON TO BOURNEMOUTH
ASHFORD TO DOVER

COUNTRY RAILWAY ROUTES
BOURNEMOUTH TO EVERCREECH JUNCTION
READING TO GUILDFORD

SOUTHERN MAIN LINES
WOKING TO PORTSMOUTH
HAYWARDS HEATH TO SEAFORD
EPSOM TO HORSHAM
CRAWLEY TO LITTLEHAMPTON
THREE BRIDGES TO BRIGHTON
WATERLOO TO WOKING
VICTORIA TO EAST CROYDON
TONBRIDGE TO HASTINGS
EAST CROYDON TO THREE BRIDGES
WOKING TO SOUTHAMPTON

STEAMING THROUGH
STEAMING THROUGH KENT
STEAMING THROUGH EAST HANTS
STEAMING THROUGH EAST SUSSEX
STEAMING THROUGH SURREY
STEAMING THROUGH WEST SUSSEX
STEAMING THROUGH THE
    ISLE OF WIGHT

OTHER RAILWAY BOOKS
WAR ON THE LINE
(Reprint of the SR history in World War II)
GARRAWAY FATHER AND SON
(Biography - includes LNER, Talyllyn and Festiniog Railways)

OTHER BOOKS
MIDHURST TOWN – THEN & NOW
EAST GRINSTEAD – THEN & NOW
THE MILITARY DEFENCE OF WEST SUSSEX
WEST SUSSEX WATERWAYS
SURREY WATERWAYS
BATTLE OVER PORTSMOUTH
A City at war in 1940
SUSSEX POLICE FORCES

*Video also available. Details from
M.P. Videos, 11 Park Crescent, Midhurst,
West Sussex GU29 9ED.*